Publisher:
Bruno Alfieri

Technical consultant:
Walter Beltrami

Editors:
Ippolito Alfieri, Silvia Giacobone

Photos:
Roberto Carrer, Gabriela Noris, Guy Mangiamele

Graphic design:
Giordano Barazzetti

Production:
Massimo Fabbri, Attilio Chiozza

Translation:
Jane Glover

INDEX

- 5   The family tree
- 13 Design
- 35 The mecanicals
- 57 Driving impressions

ISBN 88-85880-51-7   CL 41-0238-X

La Collection®
© 1992 by Automobilia Srl
Società per la Storia e l'Immagine dell'Automobile
I-20125 Milano, via Ponte Seveso 25
All rights are reserved for all countries

PRINTED AND BOUND IN ITALY
by Grafiche Editoriali Padane, Cremona, March 1992.

BMW 850i

Stefano Pasini

AUTOMOBILIA

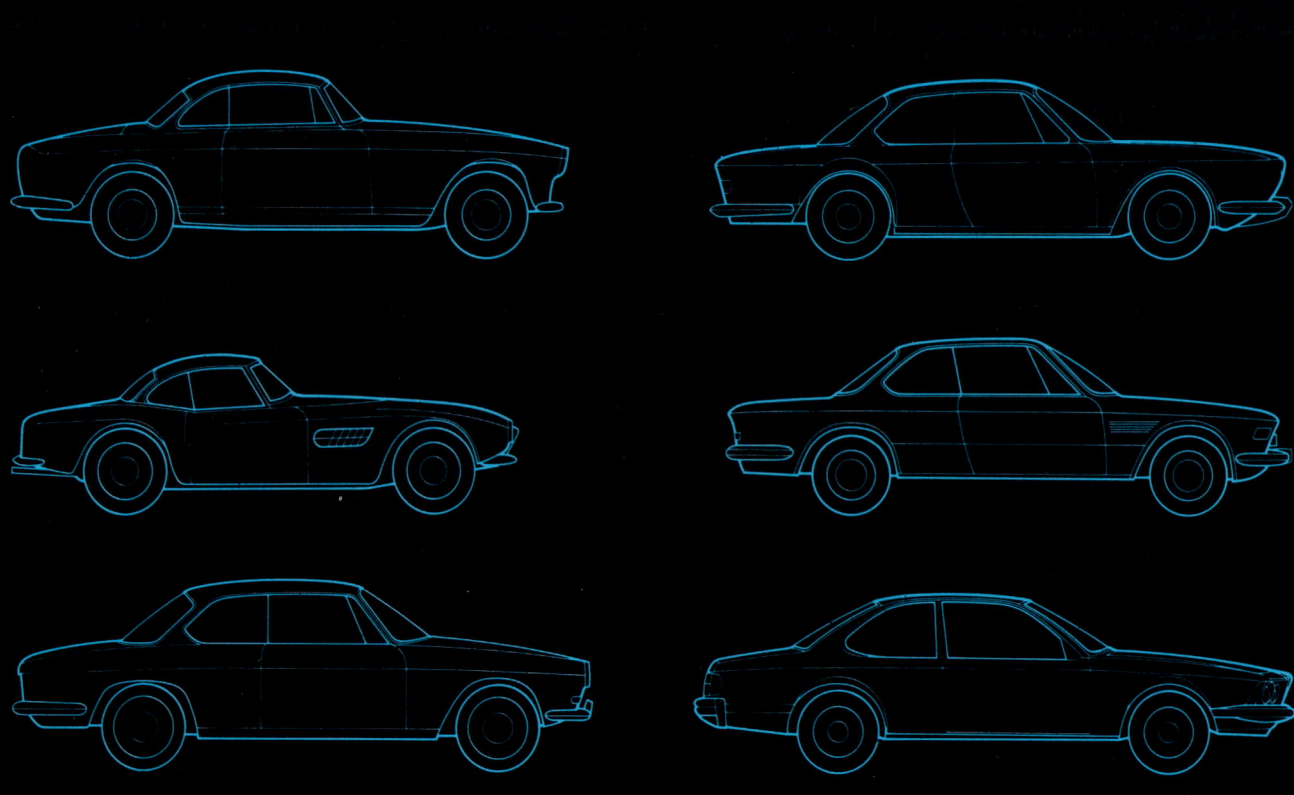

THE FAMILY TREE

Despite the prestigious position it now occupies, the BMW marque made its appearance relatively late in the history of the motor car. It was not until 1928 that it was created from a rib of the Bayerische Flugzeugwerke, a firm set up in 1916 to produce aero engines, and which had changed its name to the now familiar Bayerische Motoren Werke in 1922. Six years later BMW bought the Dixi factory in Eisenach and there started production of the modest Austin Seven under licence. Following this the Bavarian factory gradually expanded until in 1933 it introduced its first 6-cylinder model (303) and its first quality sports car, the 328, in 1936. A light car, it was a very interesting one for that period, and was driven by an inline 6-cylinder engine which became a classic, and after the war was used by Bristol in their elegant 400 and the models derived from it from 1949 onwards. The family of high-class BMW coupés was born when the firm decided to introduce a fixed-head, more tranquil sports car alongside the 328. Performance would be to some extent sacrificed in favour of the qualities of a comfortable road car with high-class bodywork. The 2-door Autenrieth coupés built on the 327 chassis were unmistakably German, original, not overfast (although 125 kph was a more than acceptable top speed for a 2-litre car in 1937), well-built, excellent travelling companions for the tourist of that period.

The Bavarian factory, guilty of being a precision engineering firm which made it a priority strategic target, was destroyed by the Second World War along with many other valuable things in Germany. After 1942 not even the excellent Focke-Wulf 190A fighters or the extraordinary Messerschmitt 262s, although they were powered by BMW engines, could protect the factory any longer from the raids by the massed formations of Allied bombers. Forced in the immediate post-war period to manufacture humble objects of all kinds in order to survive, and stripped of Eisenach which was located behind the Iron

Some of the 850i's ancestors. Left, from top to bottom: the 503, the 507 and the 3200 Cs. Right, from top to bottom: the 2000 C/Cs, the 2500 Cs and the 628 Csi.

The 328 (1936-1940). The first real production sports car built by the Bavarian firm. The first high-performance coupé came the following year, and was named the 327.

The 507 (1956-1959). An elegant, tapering roadster with a hard-top. Powered by a 3168 cc V8 engine, it had an output of 150 HP, and has remained a classic of automobile history.

curtain (and was brought back to life by the Communist regime with the EMW marque), with Teutonic tenacity BMW arose again in the 1950s. In 1951 the first of the 500 class appeared. This was the "Baroque Angels" series, from which in 1956 Baron von Goertz derived his good-looking 503 coupé. In 1955 BMW began to produce the Isetta under licence, followed by the little 600 in 1956 and the 700 from which the coupé was derived in 1960. There was a further step up in 1962 with the introduction of the 3200CS coupé, with lines which came close to the aesthetics of the big 2-door cars which were to be built by the Bavarians in the future. There was

The M1 (1978-1981). Styled by Giorgetto Giugiaro, with unmistakably Italian lines, it was somewhat different from the established BMW style. The project was originally awarded to Lamborghini, but it was concluded by BMW itself. Its 3.5-litre 6 cylinder engine provided a top speed of 262 kph, and it was built in small series.

no break in continuity, on the contrary there was a natural handover to the series of cars which followed. The discarding of the ponderous 8-cylinder engine in favour of a light 6-cylinder marked the birth of a new and even more advanced generation of BMW coupés. The series which began with the original 2000Cs, evolved with the 2800/3.0 Cs/Csi and reached its peak with the 3.0 Csi - produced from 1972-1976 - is one of the milestones in the firm's post-war development, a worthy inheritor of the historic 328. Along with its excellent sales results, in fact, this attractive class ushered back in BMW's sporty spirit, and in its several different evolutions (first and foremost the lightened Csl and the sensational Batmobile) was one of the great protagonists of the Touring Car Championships of those fiery years, collecting an impressive number of laurels. But along with its competition successes, it was the lines of the 3.0 Csi which struck the public most: low and slim, with a tapering waistline harmonising well with the generous window area above it, and elegant windows without any central pillar, this coupé established a new term of reference in the field of the Businessman's Express where up until then the English had been masters.

The story of the M1 was decidedly different: it should have been BMW's technological flagship, representative of an expanding company, demonstrating its technical and financial health, but it proved to be much less effective than had been hoped. BMW entrusted the original project to Lamborghini, who were at the time in severe financial difficulties but had an excellent technical staff who were experts in the field of extreme, rear-engined saloons

The evolution of the BMW badge. The stylised screw propeller recalls the origins of the Bayerische Motoren Werke. In the early years, its business was building aero engines.

(look at the Miura, the Urraco and the Countach). The contract was taken away because Lamborghini finished the money budgeted after completing the design project but without building the prototype. Instead of supplying further finance the Bavarians took the project and finished the car in Munich. The result was a lame super-car with a 6-cylinder engine which did not give it the cachet of the Italian super-cars with their 8 or even 12 cylinders. Neither its Latin lines not the single-marque Procar Championship were enough to place the M1 in the empyrean of the motor car to which it so openly aspired. It was, however, a fine attempt.

Scalded perhaps by the lukewarm welcome the public gave the M1, BMW went partway back in its tracks when designing the 6 Series (introduced in 1984), a true grand tourer, with two doors and room for four adults in reasonable comfort. Closely derived from the 7 Series saloon car, the new coupé had the same aesthetic imprint. The glorious 3.0 Csi had the airy lines achieved by side-windows without the B-posts.

Pretty and fast, in 3-litre and 3.3-litre straight six versions, followed by a 2.8-litre, and a 3.5 litre at the top of the "normal" range, and the M-Technik 24-valver for the most demanding customers, the 6-Series was extremely successful. It stayed in production until 1989, and during this time developed a markedly strong sports personality, with numerous international wins in the various Touring Car Championships. But at the end of the 1980s, although it was an extremely evolved product, the big coupé had revealed its development limits, and its legacy could certainly not be taken up by the controversial Z1 roadster, which at the time was at an advanced planning stage, but which was small and a rag-top.

In taking the decision to design a completely new car, a descendant of the 7-Series introduced in the second half of the 1980s, BMW decided to up the level of their flagship: to put it right at the top of its class. It was not, quite naturally, an undertaking to be approached lightly.

The 850i's closest ancestor was the M635 Csi (1984-1989), equipped with the M1-derived 6-cylinder engine.

DESIGN

The project

It was the very excellence of the cars which went before it which led the BMW management during the first half of the 1980s to provide an extremely precise brief for the new coupé. The aim was to make the new car the real jewel in Munich's crown, a top-level expression of the firm's technological ability, a love-object motivated by impeccable technical substance. All within a completely German tradition: not too adventurous, absolutely reliable, responsible, comfortable. Because it was quite clear that the big new BMW's preferred target was not to be Porsche nor Ferrari and certainly not Lamborghini: rare, exclusive objects, possessed of an undeniable allure, but also thoroughbred sports cars with a strictly limited use (and market). The new BMW's principal target, as always, was a Mercedes, the biggest coupé produced by the century-old milestone of automotive history, the same Daimler-Benz for which the Bavarians nourish a love-hate relationship which is externalised, beyond the official handshakes, in what have become non-stop bursts of technological tag, diplomatic knife-thrusts, political bullying and bare-faced price wars. At the time, from the heights of its confirmedly unique status, the Mercedes SEC had all to itself a market in which there was no place for the old 635 Csi, dated, cramped and above all with a range of engines which went no further than a 3.5-litre 6-cylinder against its Swabian rival's 5 (later 5.6) -litre 8-cylinder. To attack this powerful rival, seeing that the customer wanted more bulk, more room, more pistons and more horses than the 635 could offer, it was decided to provide him with just this, and to equip the new coupé with a single engine, the new 5-litre V12 which was at the time in an advanced stage of planning and which was destined for the 750i saloon (introduced in 1987). Having thus settled the engine question with this profluvium of pistons, the Bavarian firm unleashed its engineers to design a car to be a true and

The BMW 850i was launched at the Frankfurt Motor Show in September 1989. It is the Bavarian firm's interpretation of the Nineties sports coupé concept. From this angle the car's proportions are easily legible: wide, long and low, with a compressed nose. The only engine available is the 5-litre 12-cylinder.

Frontal three-quarter view. The well-known "twin nostril" has been restyled and also acts as a radiator air inlet. The 850i has retractable headlights for night driving, and light clusters set into the bumper.

Rear three-quarter view. Widened wheelarches suggest safety and solidness. The big, rear lights have an original design. Spoked wheels hark back to the past.

Overhead view of the rear. The roof is set well back, but the boot has a good load-carrying capacity.

explicit celebration of its technical potential.

The very nature of the coupé in the German mode, precisely the style of the SEC, immediately ruled out the technical impostation of an Italian super sports car, renouncing performance crumbs in favour of roominess and a boot: it was therefore decided to preserve the most classic of mechanical layouts, front engine, rear drive, mid-cabin. The decision to attack the market of the SEC, a car of both great opulence and comfort, eliminated right from the start any possibility of launching the new big BMWs on a victorious sporting career worthy of the old 635.

Furthermore the totally asynchronous evolution of the competition rules and the requirements of the firm's rich customers could not be reconciled in a single multipurpose model. So the defence of BMW's honour in the Touring Car Championships passed with great effectiveness to the ultra-light M3s, while their big sister turned into something quite different. In order better to signify the break with the past, whereas the new version of the saloon had kept the "7" designation (a mark of continuity which certainly did not go unappreciated by the characteristically solid buyer of these saloons), the coupé did not keep the "6" but was projected forward, and with the 5-litre engine the designation inevitably became "850", with a tiny, final "i" to signify fuel injection.

The conceptual prolegomena of this operation made it quite obvious that the flood of neuronal messages expended on the conception of the 850i were all aimed at producing a car of some considerable note. The initial decision to make it a sort of fast, mobile, shop-window for all the

Bavarian refinements meant that the 850 was born with a perfect integration of such systems on board, while the fact that the V12 was the only engine available meant that there was no need to orchestrate any compromises in favour of more proletarian engine sizes and/or cheaper models and a lower entry-level. It was quite natural that the design specifications of this coupé should call for a more sporty car than its natural rival, the Mercedes.

So the lines were tapered off to make it look less like a saloon with its back doors welded shut, and more of a true sports car (in obeisance to BMW's perennial competition aspirations), even though this cut down on back-seat comfort, and the studies which were carried out for the rear suspension alone would fill an entire book, and very probably jammed more than one computer in the celebrated FIZ Design Centre. However, all in all the new BMW flagship ended up with a design which was suited to the tastes of its natural market. Since the extremely high asking price for one of these cars was certainly not within the reach of the average young man, and given that this volume of money coupled with the desire to drive can more easily be found in a 40/50 year-old member of the professional classes, upwardly mobile and very demanding, this is the hypothetical buyer for whom the 850i was specified. It should also be taken into account that this

Overhead view of the front. The imposing bonnet, which conceals the generous 12-cylinder engine, is characterised by twin strakes converging towards the BMW grille.

forty-fifty year-old will probably have arrived at the 850i because he was looking for something more rational (i.e. more comfortable and relaxing, quieter and more obedient) than his adored Porsche Carrera, which has become too stiff and hard for him. All in all, it is the recipe which has been theorised and applied for de-

The 850i seen from the side. Note the perfectly balanced masses. There is no B-pillar: with the windows down the 850i is very exciting to look at.

cades by the aristocrats at Newport Pagnell on their Aston Martins, and which here has been reheated in a German sauce and is therefore more reliable and reasonable, with the additional guarantee of the BMW marque.

Styling

Child of an illustrious tradition of clean-limbed coupés, absolutely Germanic and unmistakably Bavarian, the 850i in no way fails to live up to expectations. If anything, it confirms their validity, elevating the qualities of its ancestors to match the firm's greatly increased power, and the consequentially weighty image which it must, and desires to, transmit. The 850i is traditionally set up, and aesthetically it oozes the solid good sense of the best German entrepreneurs. But it exists also as a manifesto of the renewed power of the firm whose marque it bears, and of the nation in which it has its roots. It is therefore a butch, muscular car, and the physical expression of its beauty is more akin to Helmut Kohl than to Claudia Schiffer. However, the image of the 850i's many qualities has been incorporated into the body design extremely effectively.

The most immediate aesthetic sign of the bond with the best of BMW traditions is right at the front of the car, where once again the twin nostrils are to be found, although this traditional marque motif is

Opposite page: frontal view. Above. Close-up of the open headlights.

Details of the badge, on the right-hand edge of the boot-lid, and of the filler cap, on the car's right side panel.

Opposite page. Rear view. The rectangular-section twin exhausts are sited to the sides.

now stylised in the extreme. A bold stroke has been to have the grille act as the bumper as well; thanks to the use of 8 kph impact-absorbing plastics it was possible to get rid of the classic bumper blade, and the advantage is that of a nose with much cleaner lines. This means that the 850i's wedge-shaped impetus starts right from the front, which is as tapered as a Ferrari without being as vulnerable. The decision to go with this very slim type of grille-bumper combination is also a consequence of the desire to keep the bonnet low for aesthetic and aerodynamic reasons. This meant that in order to have headlights high enough off the ground to meet the minimum requirements of certain national regulations (read USA), the designers had to resort to pop-up headlights, which is uncommon for the Bavarians. In addition it meant insertion of the beam headlights and the hazard lights into the depths of this unusual bumper, along with the indicators, providing a wealth of reflectors and glazed areas which is characteristic of the most advanced supercars.

Alongside the wide bonnet the wheelarches reveal an obvious concession to certain German preferences, with their robust blister-like swellings. These are generally distinctive traits of transformation jobs done by preparers like AMG, Alpina, Koenig, etc., who enlarge the bodywork to lodge the widest of tyres,

suited to the conspicuous injection of power. The transfer here is obvious, swollen wheelarches become an immediate guarantee of this additional power.

They are pleasing in this elegant body, because they give movement to a flank which would otherwise be too smooth and decidedly monotonous, and they also communicate a reassuring message of power dressed to kill.

Another link with the best of BMW tradition, one which most distinctly states that the 850i belongs to the elite family of the Bavarian coupés, can be seen in the pillarless side windows; there is no sign of the upright which in more modest cars would be between the front and rear door windows. As we saw earlier, its absence had already become a distinctive detail of the various "Cs", was perpetuated in the "6", and is once more proposed here on the wave of success which it enjoyed previously. The lack of the central B-post gives the cabin a unique airness, especially when the side windows are lowered, and in so doing all links with the aesthetics of a saloon car are erased. It is, moreover, a game which only becomes reasonable when the necessary technology is available, so that there are no consequences to abolishing the central upright. The fact that both airtightness and watertightness have to be ensured by two mobile windows in contact with each other

The roof panel is light, allowing an ample glassed area. On this page, two close-ups of the boot showing the tool kit and the spare-wheel housing.

The practical dashboard, with its well-placed, easily legible, instruments. The coupling of the tacho with the speedometer is an original feature.

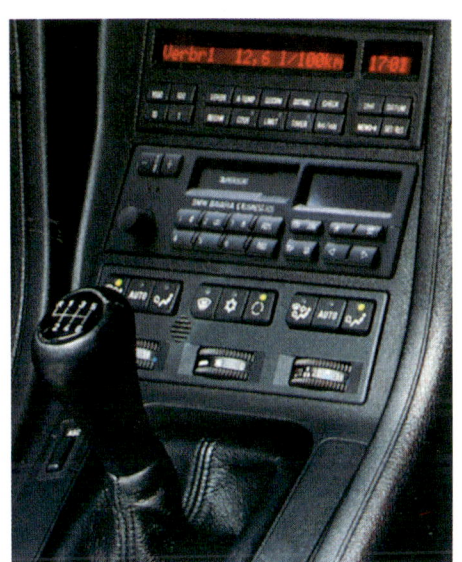

Close-up of the central console, with the on-board computer and the gearstick of the 6-speed manual unit.

The 850i has integral seatbelts (SGS). This solution has numerous advantages for safety, the most important of which is the permanent optimal geometry of each belt, regardless of seat position.

Centre. The front seats. Upholstery is available in five types of velvet, 12 types of leather and two types of buffalo hide. Below. The rear seats. The 850i is a 4-seater car.

Close-up of the arm-rest on the driver's side, with the controls for the door mirrors, windows and central locking.

windows fitted flush to the body and the windscreen wipers half hidden behind the back edge of the bonnet confer a modern look without any extremes in the avant-garde mode. All this also assists the car's aerodynamic efficiency which is officially declared as an excellent Cx of 0.29. The same considerations are true of the tail styling, where the lines of the metal sheets are dry, taut and essential. Luckily there are neither aerodynamic strakes or stabilisers, but the line of the rear light clusters has a curiously tormented look along the bottom edge, something for which it is rather difficult to understand the reason. But overall, even an inspection of the individual parts cannot but confirm the impressions of the 850i's excellent design - on which is proudly displayed one of the most graphically attractive marques in the world, the stylised depiction of a rotating aeroplane propeller, with the stroboscopic segments painted in the white and blue of Bavaria.

There are other connections with BMW styling, such as the graphics of the name on the rear, in a chromium plated metal badge placed on the right-hand side of a volumetrically unmistakable tail; the star-shaped rims, in which one can pick out either twelve "hollowed out" spokes or 24 single but very fine ones. It is impossible, when talking about styling, to ignore the aesthetic finish of the engine: in its bay

instead of being in strong, fixed frames, invests the quality of the central seal and the different movement with capital importance. This is why Mercedes can do it, BMW can do it, but when the English tried (the Jaguar XJC) it was a disaster.

The side mirrors are well-integrated into the overall lines of the body. The

which excellent wiring has left clean, the big V12 is dominated by the black air-filter complex with its BMW badge, and this is crowned by the 12 exhaust conduits. Very pretty, but you do tend to think about how much stuff has to be removed before you can change a plug. Finally, the interior. Well-designed, well-matched, and essential lines which harmonise well with the taste of the exterior. The seats are of excellent design and all the instrumentation is rationally set out. The 850i meets extremely high technical and aesthetic requirements in a modern style which is extremely functional and gives away little to useless ornament or decoration. The main instrument console is well made, although the placing of the speedometer above the rpm counter is a dubious one. Lighting is excellent, the positioning of minor controls is good and the controls on the steering column for the lights, wipers, etc. are well made (with a definite touch of "BMW familiarity").

Perhaps the one thing which comes closest to a gratuitous gizmo in this sober cabin is the petulant signalling of service intervals, which is an insult to the intelligence of the customer of a machine like this, who is by definition both a connoisseur and discriminating. Let us hope that sooner or later they decide to eliminate it; the dry "good Gestalt" of all the other instruments deserves it.

The controls for the electrically adjustable seats, with a 3-position memory. They are set on the outside of the seat bases.

THE MECHANICALS

The BMW 850i is a 2-seater sports coupé, front engine, rear boot, with 2+2 interior. The gears are in unit with the engine, it has rear drive, and the body is a steel monocoque. The project has a rather conventional basis therefore, and there is little change from what has already been applied by the big Italian and English manufacturers in course of the last three decades. Where the 850i excels is in the application of state of the art technology and of its enormous industrial capabilities to this kind of elite motor car. Something which is amply demonstrated when the car is examined in detail.

The engine is the real heart of this car, and this is underlined by the choice of such a high number of cylinders. Here more than anywhere else lies the indication of that will to beat the competition which BMW demonstrates with this product, while the high engine displacement and the resulting power on tap reveals its global aims. With characteristic German rationality, this 12-cylinder renounces the more intricate timing systems which are a typical feature of Italian-built cars, adopting instead a more linear style which has each bank of cylinders served with a chain-driven single overhead camshaft, with hydraulic rocker arms operating the valves (the exhaust valves are sodium-cooled, converging at the top of the combustion chamber at a very acute angle, to optimize the flow of the mixture).

The engine block construction is extremely interesting. It was designed with the aim of achieving compactness, especially in height, in order to fit the large V12 easily under the coupé's tapering nose. Since moreover weight and wear were also of primary importance, it was decided to cast the monoblock in a sophisticated metal alloy (AlSil6Cu4Mg). Secondary processing of the cylinder linings leaves nothing but silicon crystals on the surface, thereby optimizing the piston movement. Simpler metallurgy for the driveshaft which is in CK45 steel, providing maximum torsional and flexural effici-

The 850i with its bonnet up. The generous cooling plant, completely faired-in, stands out in the foreground. One is struck straightaway by the strict, typically Germanic, tidiness with which each mechanical organ has been placed.

The 850i's 60° V cylinder block is all-light alloy, with in-block liners. Right-hand page, lateral view of the cylinder heads and manifolds.

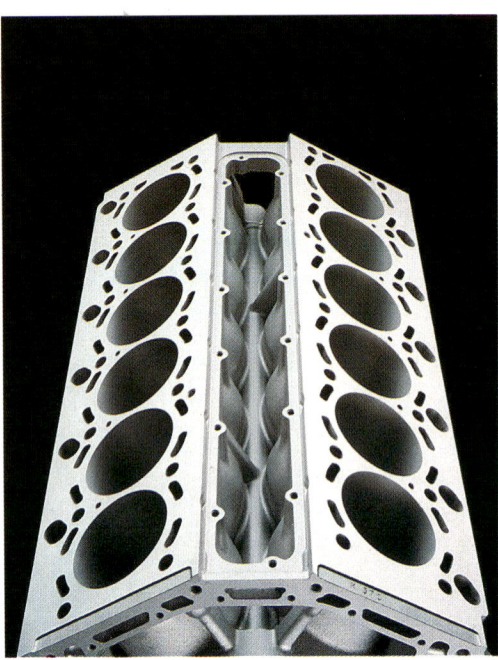

ency. The connecting rods are identical to those on the well-known 2.5 litre inline six (525i, 325i). Naturally the coolant and lubrication circuits have been improved to meet the requirements of a powerful 5-litre which for aerodynamic reasons has been allowed only relatively small air intakes, although the performance figures demanded are quite high. In particular, the oil supply is a critical input for the effective working of an engine with hydraulically operated valves, and the fitting of a thermostatically-controlled oil radiator is an additional guarantee. In the same way the drive belts and pulleys of the secondary systems (air conditioning, etc.) have been improved to the point of being declared as "maintenance free". The aspiration plant also has some interesting details, such as conduits of exactly the same length for each of the 12 cylinders, and an electronic valve for engine regulation (EML). A disc filter cleans the intake air before it divides for the two banks of cylinders. The fully electronic ignition is operated by a micro-processor, and has two identical DME 1.7 management systems, one for each cylinder bank.

These engine managers perform multiple functions, e.g. anti-knocking, cold-starting, pre-heating of the Lambda probe, mapped ignition, emergency programmes (with the possibility of "limping home": if there should be a problem in

one half of the engine, the other half will get the car home anyway) and self diagnostic functions which store any malfunctions in the memory. The dual section 3-way ceramic catalyser reduces neither engine output nor torque.

The exhaust plant terminates with two pipes located symmetrically under the rear bumper, with a square section which copies the same distinctive mark of the 750i, and as such should be read as a symbol of nobility.

Two versions of the gearbox are available in the 850i. The first one is the 4-speed automatic (4HP-24EH), electro-hydraulically operated, and with a locking torque convertor: this is exactly the same as the one fitted in the 750i, and there are three functioning modes to choose from: "E", "S", "M". The "E" position is for economic running, "S" for sporty driving with higher speed changes, and "M" prevents unwanted automatic gearchanges with a locking system. With its own diagnostics system and a memory, the automatic gearbox is a modern and effective mechanism.

Obviously, the manual 6-speed gearbox is more sporty, with a very stiff sump, and the abundance of ratios has been chosen as an aid to fluid driving. It has innovative synchromesh on all gears, using ATF (automatic transmission fluid) which makes for ease of movement even with cold starting. The box is mounted between the engine and the chassis on a front bearing and a transversal support in order to guarantee better uncoupling of the

Opposite page. The M70 engine in the 850i's front bay. This generous 300 HP engine also powers the 750, the top model in the prestigious 7-Series. Various auxiliary parts had to be moved around in order to fit the engine into the 850.

Left. An interesting illustration of the 12 pistons, showing the combustion chamber, partly formed inside the crown of the piston.

Engine cross section. Each bank of cylinders is managed by a separate Bosch Motronic injection/ignition controller. This means that each bank works as an independent 6-cylinder engine.

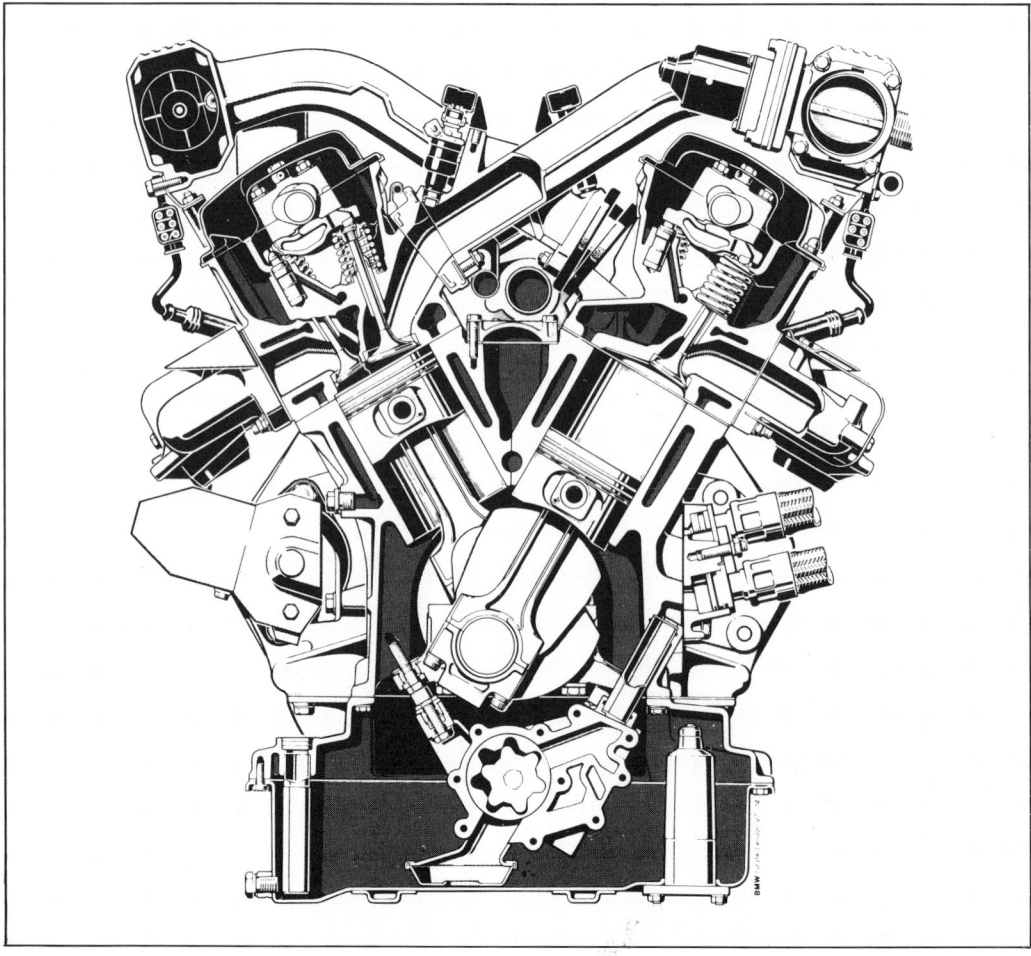

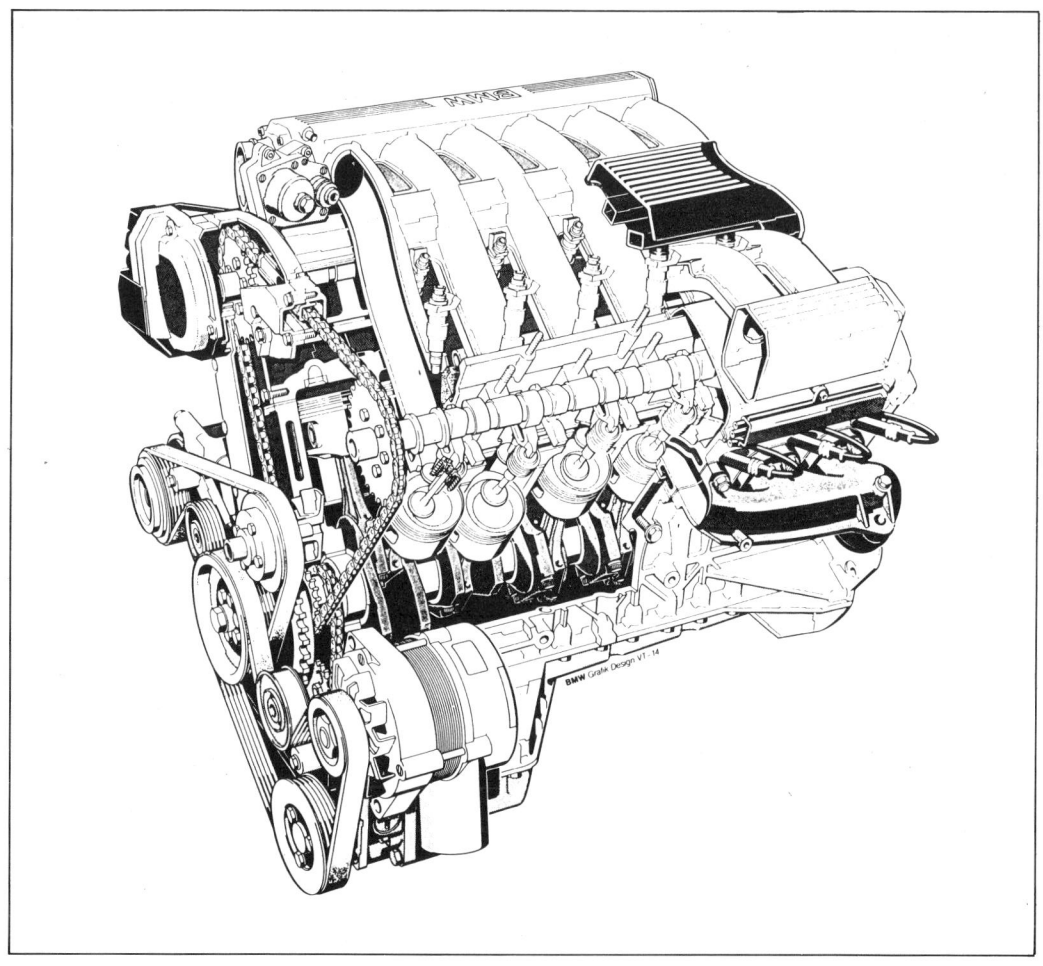

Section plane of the engine. Timing is of the traditional 2-valve type, with chain-driven camshaft and hydraulic valve play control.

This drawing illustrates the behaviour of a car fitted with ASC (automatic stability control) and one without (below). The advantages to be gained from this system in emergency conditions are well illustrated.

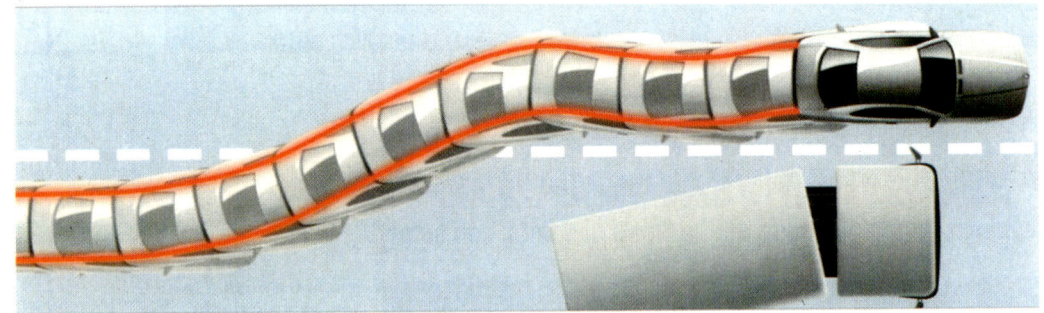

bodywork. Thanks to the engine's 300 HP, the 850i has a theoretical top speed which probably tops 270 kph, but this is limited by the manufacturer in line with a German auto-disciplinary code to 250 kph. This speed is reached in 6th gear at only 5200 rpm.

BMW have made an interesting innovation on the evolved version of the manual gearbox, with what they call ASC+T, standing for automatic stability control by intervention on propulsive torque. This is an evolution of the current system on the 7-Series and on the 850i automatic, where in rear wheel slip is regulated by reducing the opening of the throttle only. In its most complete version, which is only applied on the 850i with the manual gearbox, this operation is completed by the simultaneous modification of the ignition diagram and the operation of the rear brakes (acting together with the anti-locking system).

The "cold" part of the mechanicals also demonstrates the heights of the technical and industrial abilities of the Bavarian maker. The 850i's rigid monocoque has been fitted with state of the art BMW suspensions. At the front there is an evolved version of the usual double-jointed strut, lower transverse arm and push rods, but it is at the rear, traditionally the Achilles' heel of this type of coupé, that the firm's engineers have concentrated their efforts. A detailed study of the tasks and the stresses which are required from the rear axle concluded with the design of a system which broke up into individual tasks the work it has to do (springing, wheel positioning, counteracting pitching, resistance to braking loads, etc.) in order to deal with each of these tasks in the best way possible. Making use of very advanced elastokinematic technology, the resulting design was of a five arm system linked to each wheel (three transverse and one longitudinal), linked by a fifth integral arm which, although it is materially intricate, concretely simplifies the system's functioning. This functioning is complex: I

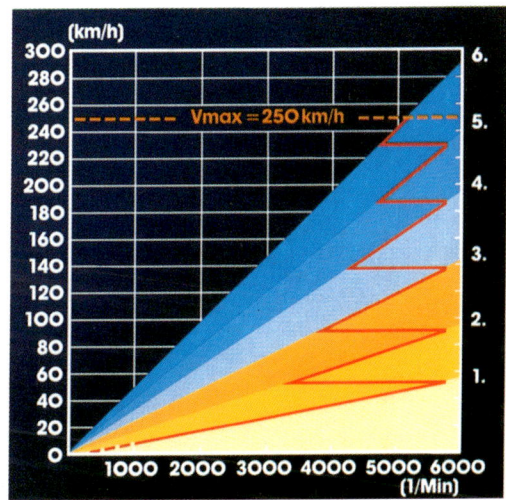

Diagram showing the top speeds attainable in each of the six gears of the manual gearbox unit. Top speed is self-limiting at 250 kph.

The 850i's Multilink rear suspension. A decided improvement in roadholding and driving precision on bends has been added to high stability in the straight and braking. This is thanks to active rear axle kinematics (AHK) - an exceptional, newly conceived option, which aids the driver with active rear-wheel steering.

The front axle. Double-jointed strut with dampers and coaxial coil springs. Self-venting disc brakes.

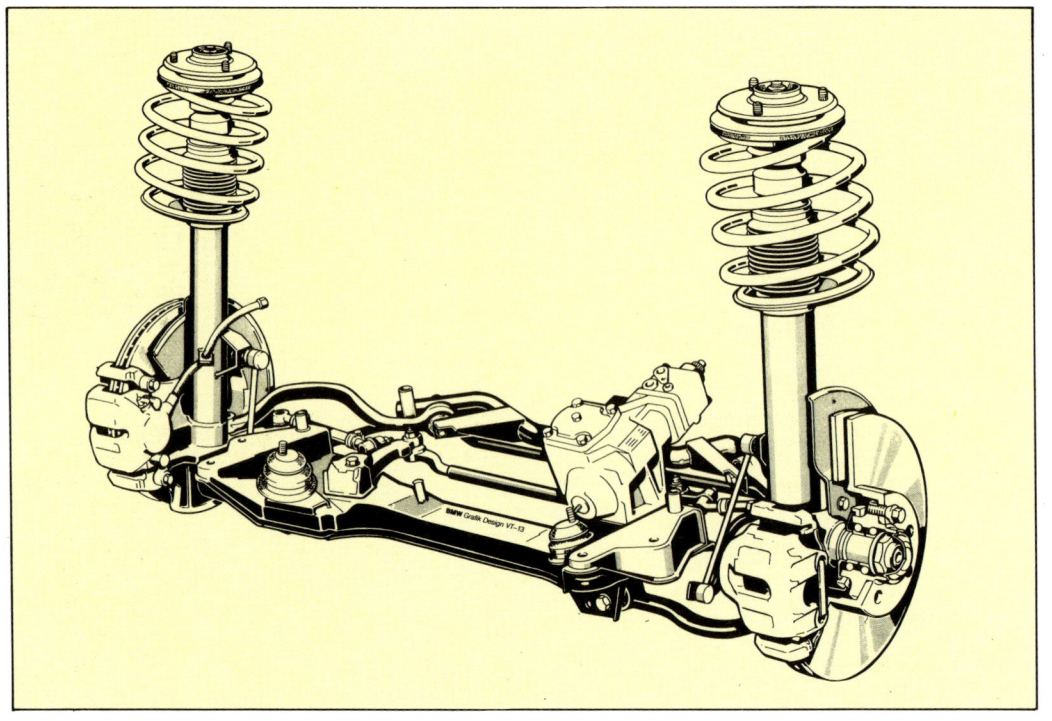

shall simplify it here by pointing out that the vertical loads (springing) are absorbed by the transverse arms, which work differentially to take care of the lateral loads too (wheel adherence on bends); loads due to acceleration torque and braking are taken care of by the push rods and the longitudinal arms. Whereas on the one hand this subdivision of the tasks of the suspension into different sub-tasks, each entrusted to specialised kinematisms, complicates the structure of the rear suspension, on the other it is an effective guarantee of a top-level result.

This complex "team" work produces an effect which was intended when the com-

Rear axle. Multilink suspension with dampers and separate coil springs. Disc brakes.

plex elastokinematic system was being designed: this is a "passive steering", as it is commonly called effect of the rear wheels. This confers a modest but significant self-steering effect on the rear wheels, which further improves the already high level of the 850i's roadholding. An active system of rear-wheel steering is available on request. Active rear axle kinematics consistently continues the various chassis and suspension innovations already introduced by BMW in the past: ABS anti-lock brakes in 1979 and ASC Automatic Stability Control in 1988.

This is the right place to mention the specific nature of trim calibration: the 850i

Diagram showing the components of the active rear axle kinematics.

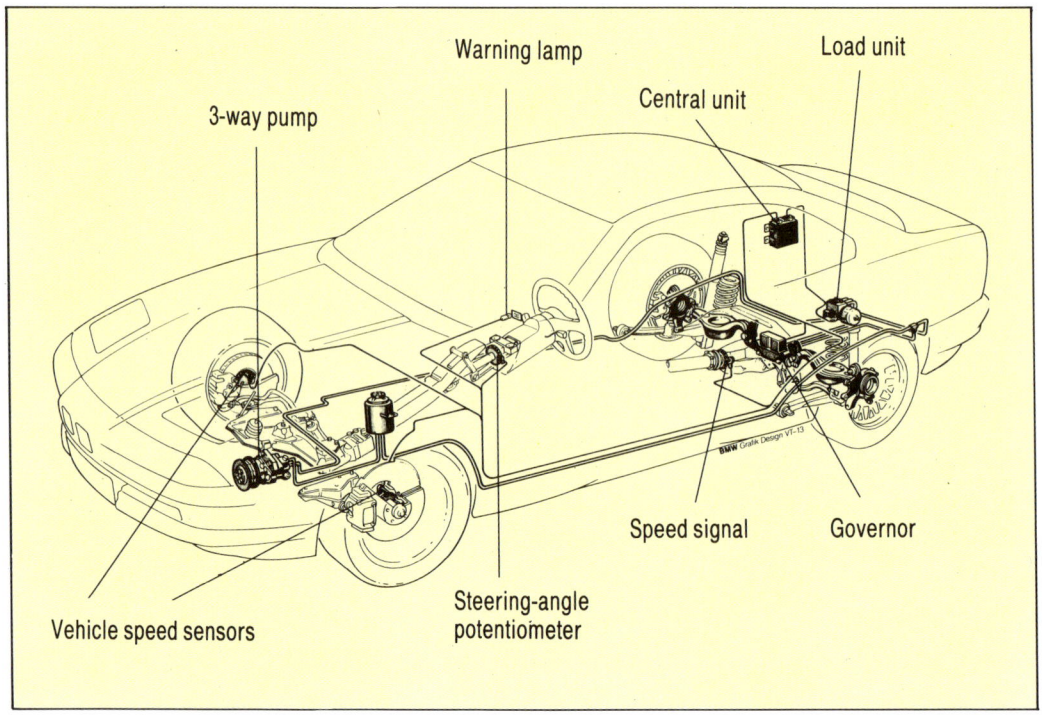

is normally supplied in the sporty set up in the case of the manual version, and the "comfortable" trim in the automatic version. But the customer will be able to order the combination best suited to his needs without any difficulty. There is a further option of EDC (electronic damping control) available as well as electronic servo-assisted steering (Servotronic).

The braking system, of course, is the most powerful and effective possible: four 32.4 cm discs with fixed calipers and asbestos-free pads with twice the friction of the last 635 Csi. The latest generation of ABS is standard, integrated as I mentioned before with the ASC+T traction control.

Tyres are generously wide, 235/50 ZR-16 on 7.5Jx16" "starred" alloy rims.

The 850i is full of other interesting structural details. One is the study done on the rubber door seals - with their upside-down "U" profile providing effective air- and watertightness in the absence of the normal fixed frame. However, as this system would present an obstacle when opening the door, when the door-lock is operated the side window automatically lowers a few millimetres, stays in this position while the door is open, and then rises automatically, slipping back under the seal on closure. Another detail worth mentioning is the adoption of Multiplex technology, a system which transmits several messages along a single electrical cable, thereby reducing the complexity of the wiring along the length of the car body, and improving transmission. The climatisation system is also very interesting. It is a complete and sophisticated system, with precise and continuous automatic temperature control which also, and this is the interesting part, continually filters the air drawn into the cabin, something which is increasingly necessary in view of the growth in atmospheric pollution and the progressive rise in any type of respiratory allergies.

Obviously, the attention BMW have paid to safety plays a very important part in this titanic effort to produce a car representing a manifesto of excellence which brooks no argument. Not just active safety, which as we have seen is taken care of here by the quality of the chassis, brakes, engine, gearbox and suspensions, but also the more brutally passive safety - the safety which is bound up with the protection a car will provide for its occupants in the event

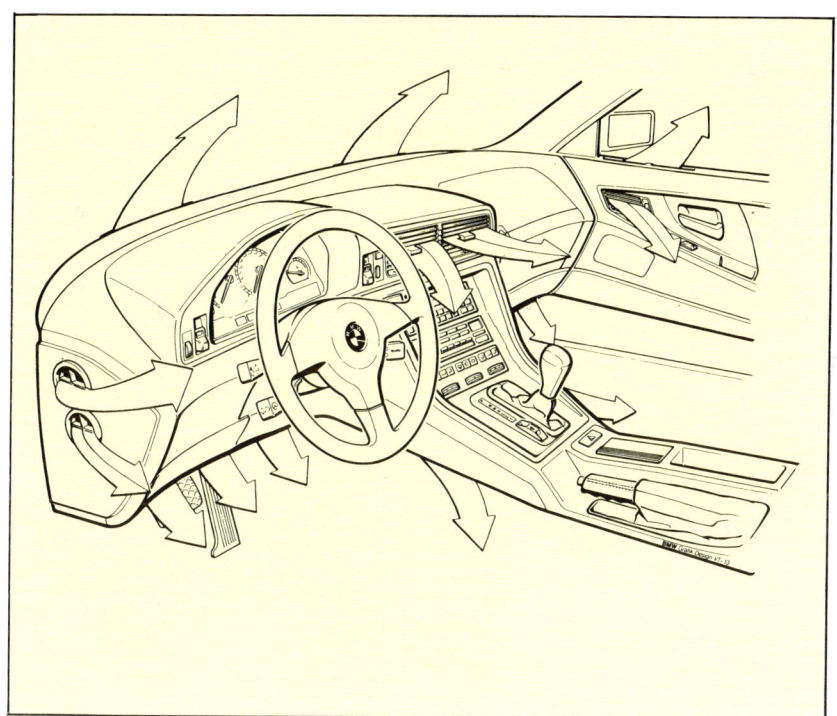

Diagram of the 850i's heating/ventilation airflows.

Special attention has been given to problems connected with safety. This illustration is of the 850i's monocoque, designed to provide high resistance in lateral impacts too.

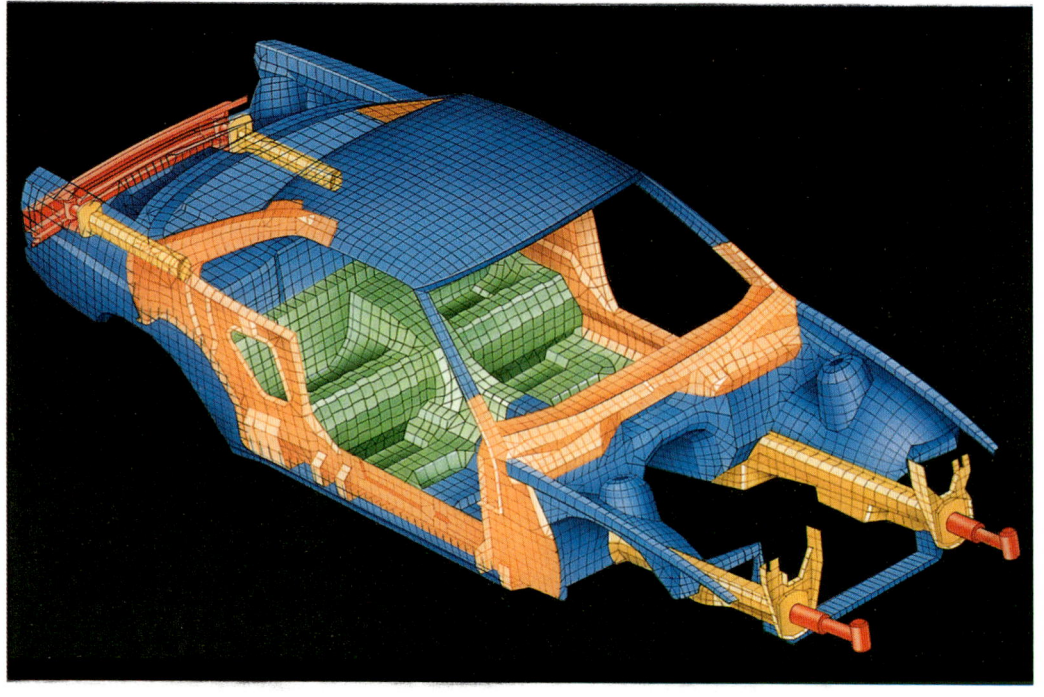

of an impact. The work carried out by the Bavarian firm in this field is exemplary, and notwithstanding the absence of the lateral reinforcement provided by the central pillar, the heavy 850i easily passes all impact tests, saving the occupants from all but the most minor damage possible, thanks to the stiffened monocoque and the careful studies into impact energy absorption along the monocoque's planned absorption areas.

A further contribution to the overall safety of this most important of BMWs comes from the advanced technology used in the design of the integral safety belts fitted both front and back. This sy-

X-ray of the 850i, highlighting the engine, transmission and rear axle.

stem is similar to the one already successfully fitted in the Mercedes-Benz SL, and is a consequence of the unsuitability of the belt's upper anchorage point in a car without a central roof pillar and with a relatively low waistline. However, it also produces considerable benefits, in that it forms a firmly integrated seat/passenger/belt grouping with consequently less possibility of separation (and therefore loss of safety) in a crash. This is of capital importance for the maximum protection of the occupants within a superbly protected environment such as that of the 850i.

The cockpit

1. Direction indicator lever, parking lights, low-beam lights and flashing.
2. Light switch.
3. Horn button.
4. Fog light switch.
5. Rear heated window switch.
6. Milled turning wheel for headlight adjustment.
7. Display with multiple information (MID).
8. Emergency flashing switch.
9. Windscreen wiper and washer lever.
10. Automatic speed-governor lever.
11. Steering wheel electric adjustment lever.
12. Bonnet opening lever.

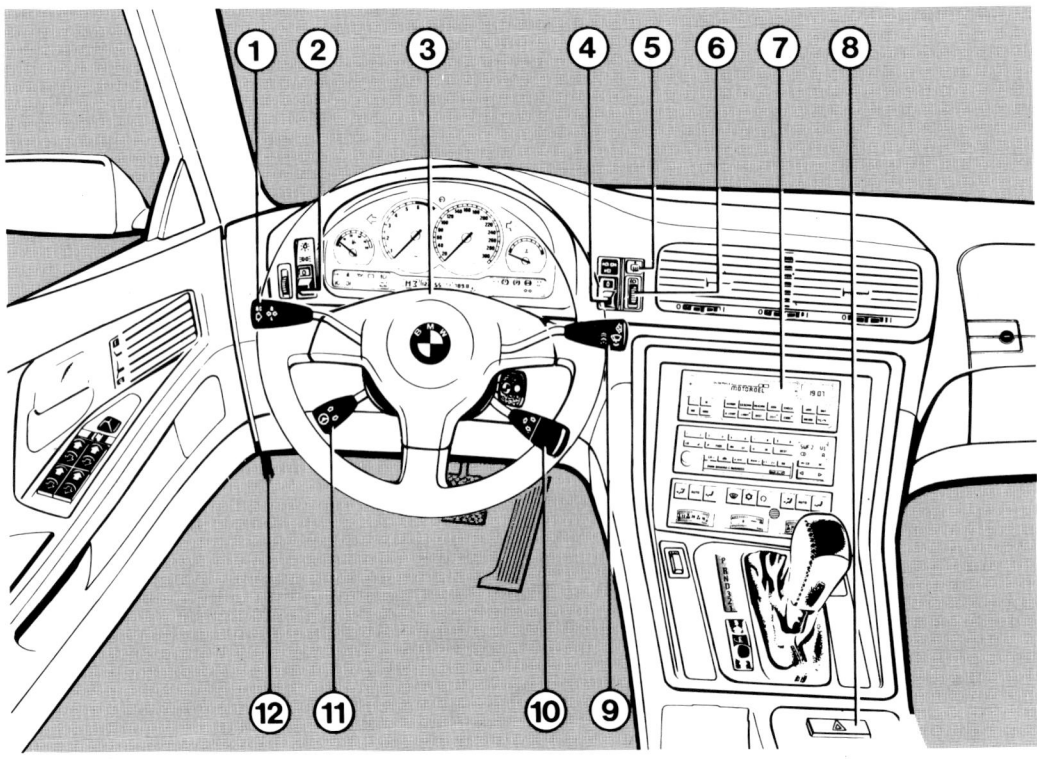

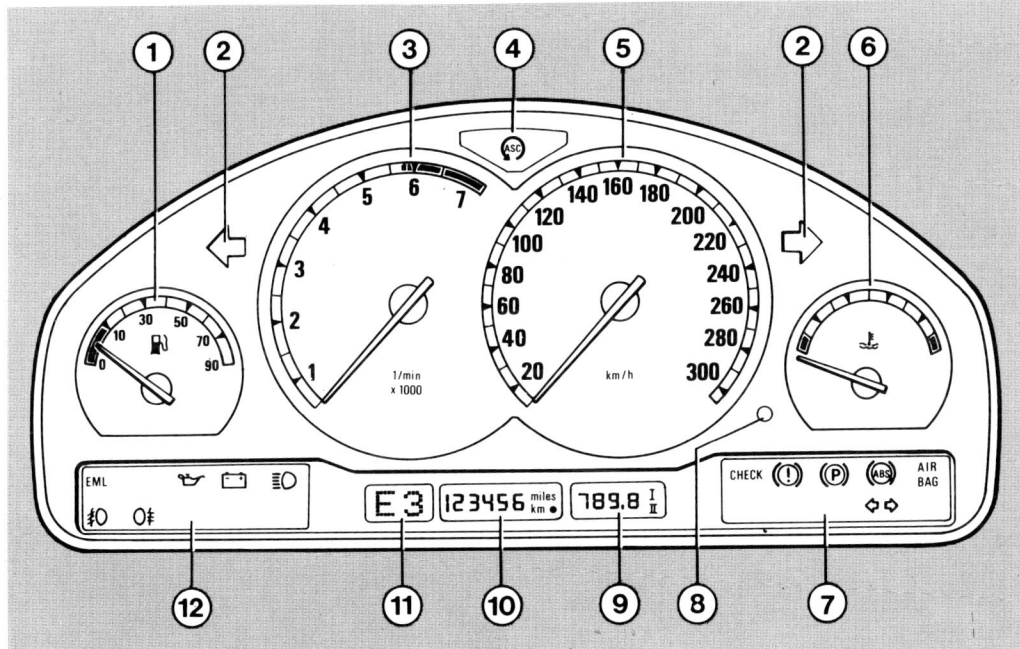

Combined instrumentation

1. Fuel level gauge with reserve warning light.
2. Direction warning lamp.
3. Rev counter.
4. ASC/ASC+T warning lamp.(*)
5. Speedometer.
6. Fridge telethermometer.
7. Check Control warning lamp; hydraulic system, brakes and steering warning lamps; handbrake; ABS; Airbag; towing flashing indicator.
8. Push-button for the trip odometer and switch for another trip odometer.
9. Trip odometer.
10. Odometer.
11. Program indicator and authomatic gear-lever position.
12. Warning lamps for engine power electronic adjustment (EML), engine oil pressure, charge of the battery, high-beam lights, foglights, rear foglights.

(*) ASC = Automatic control of stability
ASC+T = Automatic control of stability + drive

ENGINE

Disposition: front logitudinal
Materials: light alloy cylinder head and crankase
Cylinders: V12 60°
Bore and stroke: 84 x 75 mm (3.30 x 2.95 in)
Piston displacement: 4988 cc (304.51 cu in)
Compression ratio: 8.8:1
Maximum power: 220 kW (300 HP) at 5200 rpm
Maximum torque: 450 Nm (45.9 kgm) at 4100 rpm
Timing system: SOHC, 2 valves per cylinder
Fuel and ignition: electronic DME M 17
Lubrication: forced-feed
Cooling system: light alloy radiator
Emission control system: 2 3-way catalytic converters and Lambda sensor (USA '83)

DRIVELINE

Drive: rear-wheel
Clutch: dry single-plate
Gearbox: automatic, 4-speed + Rev; manual, 6-speed + Rev (on request)
Gear ratios: automatic, 1st = 2.48, 2nd = 1.48, 3rd = 1.00, 4th = 0.73, Rev = 2.09; manual, 1st = 4.25, 2nd = 2.53 3rd = 1.68, 4th = 1.24, 5th = 1.00, 6th = 0.83, Rev = 3.89
Final ratio: automatic 3.15, manual 2.93
Differential: self-locking

CAR BODY

Type: 2-door coupé, 4 seats
Frame: monocoque with steel subframes
Front suspensions: double pivot spring strut with caster angle offset, lateral force compensation, brake dive reduction.
Rear suspensions: integral axle, multi-dimensional suspension on 5 track control arms, squat and brake dive compensation, anti-roll bar.
Steering system: ball and nut, hydraulic power steering $\varnothing$ 11.5 m
Brakes: self-ventilated discs, $\varnothing$ 324 mm, double circuit, ABS
Rims: 7.5J x 16
Tyres: 235/50 ZR 16
Fuel tank: 90 l (19.8 imp. gal.)

DIMENSIONS AND WEIGHTS:

Length: 4780 mm (188.1 in)
Width: 1855 mm (74.2 in)
Height: 1340 mm (52.7 in)
Wheelbase: 2684 mm (105.6 in)
Front and rear tracks: 1554/1562 mm (61.1/61.4 in)
Kerb weight: 1790 kg (3942 lbs)
Luggage capacity: 360 dm^3

PERFORMANCE

Top speed: 250 kph (155 mph)
Acceleration from 0 to 100 kph: 7.4 (manual 6.8) sec
1 km from standing start: 27.0 (manual 26.3) sec
Pick-up (from 80 to 120 kph): 6 sec
Speed per 1000 rpm: 48.9 kph
Braking distance (140 kph): 83.7 m (91.5 yd)
Consumption at 90/120/Urban Cycle: 8.6/10.3/19.8 l/100 km (manual 8.8/10.4/19.4 l/100 km)
Pass-by noise (at 120 kph): 66.5/67.5 Db front/rear
Specific power: 60.1 HP/liter (0.98 HP/cu in)
Weight to power ratio: 5.96 kg/HP (13.14 lbs/HP)

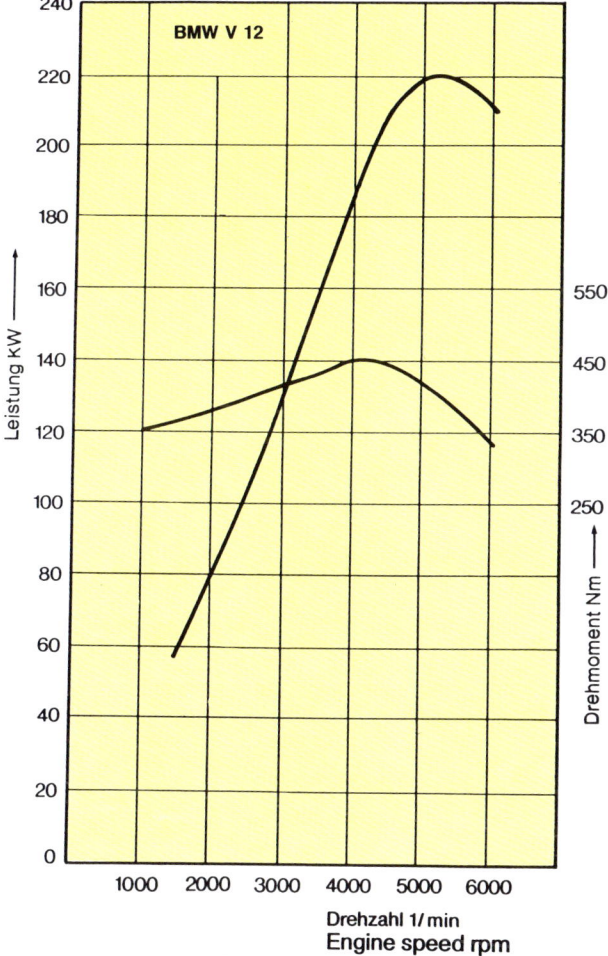
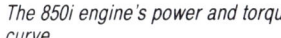

The 850i engine's power and torque curve.

DRIVING IMPRESSIONS

This is a big car when seen on the ground. Massive, even: low and wide, muscular at the wheelarches but as slim as the nose of an anteater at the front of the bonnet. Notwithstanding this, the visual compaction of the areas is admirable, and it is hard to appreciate its conspicuous dimensions. Yet 4.78 metres from bow to stern is no joke, and furthermore the 1,855 millimetres' width is a little bit of a tight fit in the winding streets of a historic town centre which, perversely, is where most of the bars in front of which one would want to show off this kind of car are located. But it is pretty. Certainly, there are those for whom it will recall Wayne Cherry's best work, but that is by no means a defect, and anyway a rapid glance is all that is needed to identify it immediately as a real, rich and rapid BMW. So one need have no doubts or identity crises when climbing aboard the most important 2+2 ever built by the Bavarians.

It is delightful to get into the car and admire the whim which has the door window automatically slide down a few millimetres to allow the door to be opened, only to rise and slide under the soft rubber seal as soon as the door is closed again, sealing it against draughts, water and noise. Once inside the 850i is exactly what one would expect from the most expensive BMW: a sobre interior, very rational, without trimmings, with a simple, not over-decorated, dashboard (good), an instrument panel with nothing but the essential instruments (very good), plenty of warning lights all of which are usually off (even better). The siting of the speedo over the tacho is rather unattractive though, the steering wheel is passable, but the transmission tunnel protrudes a little into the driver's space. The seats on the other hand are wonderful, upholstered in excellent leather (available in no colour except black however), and above all they have integral seat belts. This frees one from the slavery of searching for belts located behind the door line, and also from the interfering little arm which presents

In line with an agreement between BMW, Mercedes and Audi, the 850i has a top speed of 250 kph. Without the limiter, (estimated) top speed would be around 280 kph.

More than the Italian GTs, the 850i's competitors are the German sports coupés, such as the Porsche 928 and the Mercedes SEC: high performance with high-level driving comfort.

the seat belt every time one gets back into the SEC. The front seats are excellent and roomy, with an excellent adjustment range for both the seats and the steering wheel. There is very good all-round visibility thanks to the classic lines and the generous amount of window area. The seats behind are much less roomy, and their existence could quite happily be forgotten if the world did not contain small dogs, cars and even children under the age of five and three feet who, once slotted into their relative cubicles, might perhaps be able to breathe.

As far as humans anywhere over this size are concerned, you can forget the en-

The driver has optimal conditions of active safety, thanks to the 850i's sophisticated electronic control systems. Naturally, this in no way limits driving freedom.

thusiastically declared 2+2. But perhaps the "+2" refers to the two suitcases which, with some difficulty, it is possible to squeeze in if necessary.

The engine starts with the characteristic, elastic readiness of the modern Bavarian V12, and starts to idle with nothing more than a very distant suggestion of a buzz, more or less the same as a 320 which only has half the number of cylinders.

Naturally, immediately after ignition the automatic version is totally different from the manual version, otherwise known in a curious transfer, as "mechanical" (?). I'll take the manual first: the clutch is relatively gentle, first gear on the left, a touch of gas,

The self-steering rear wheels mean that the car enters the bend neutrally, providing conditions of absolute safety and comfort.

and the car moves off without any fuss and I run right through the gates on the gearbox, right up to sixth, both to get used to them and to test the much-declaimed docility of this enormous engine. It is, in fact, true. This V12 purrs if you stroke the gas pedal, hauling the 850i's mass in a pleasantly smooth manner. This sweetness, added to the excellent external visibility and the easily operated controls, to some extent thwarts the declared need for a six-ratio gearbox: with this kind of torque half as many gears would have been quite adequate. However, apart from the huge outer measurements, the 850i instills considerable confidence right from the first. A

The result of a prolonged project study, the 850i, with its Cx of 0.29, is one of the most aerodynamically efficient coupés on the market.

more determined pressure on the accelerator produces the desired increase in speed, and all of a sudden things get faster, impromptu, entertaining. Never rough! the engine and chassis are too well behaved to transmit anything in the realms of violence to the driver, and the super comfortable cabin filters out what miniscule amount might have managed to get through the tight diplomatic mesh of BMW's mechanical perfection. Certainly one misses (but it is by choice) the additional thrill which comes from the added vibration, from the more audible exhaust, from any of those more hormonal, animal-esque, qualities which the 850i, on the other hand, disdainfully denies in the name of finishing and of progress. It has to be said that even for 300 HP (such is the output of the big V12) moving 1,790 kg is something of a burden, and the fact that the 850i reveals a decided brilliance in sporty driving is a definite tribute to the fullness of the engine's torque curve.

This is even truer of the automatic version of the car, which is definitely an aluminium fist in a very velvety glove. Silky, beautifully behaved, this transmission really shows its intrinsic character when used at cruising speeds in the "E" position, when the 850i minimises hisses and growls until it almost seems to be a sailing boat. Fuel consumption also returns to acceptable figures for those of us who do not own Kuwait, or are, at the very least, majority shareholders in Exxon. In the "S" mode the odd jerk does filter through; nothing important for a decisive increase in acceleration, but for anyone who wants to play with the V12's 300 HP then the manual option is almost inevitable. Because the infamous ASC+T is only available in the complete form when twinned with the 6-speed gearbox. Certain so-called "experts" have come down very heavily against this traction control system, but in fact it is an excellent way of insuring oneself against the worst kind of surprises on dangerous surfaces and therefore extremely useful. In homage to the petulant flatfeet who despise the ASC+T, who are perhaps the same top-quality brains who look down from other pulpits on the Porsche Tiptronic and Carrera 4, it can be switched off, but after a certain amount of testing, one realises that it is a great advantage to have it and to leave it perennially switched on for the greater mutual protection of man and machine.

Roadholding is excellent anyway, and if the 850i's volume combined with its remarkable retail price does not tempt the driver into treating the massive autostrada bends too lightly on wet surfaces, then the car stays solidly anchored to the ground. The complicated 5-point rear suspension is revealed to be an truly excellent innovation, not just as a sheet anchor for the

Notwithstanding its 1790 kg, thanks to the 300 HP of its generous 12-cylinder, the 850i demonstrates excellent acceleration and pickup.

journalist-riveter class, and the brakes do their job faithfully and efficiently, just as they were planned to do.

Naturally, the 850i is very comfortable. The main reason for this comfort is the perfect seats. The distances and the relationship between these seats, the steering wheel, the pedals and the dimensions of the cabin have been excellently studied, and are the result of solid ergonomic research. The servo assists do their bit in alleviating the effort of driving; most of all the wheel is a real pleasure both when cruising and when driving more briskly, as well of course as when turning and parking the car (during which the tail is well placed but the bonnet less so - low, smooth and with a rake which is critical to good sighting). The low level of noise pollution inside the cabin is another factor in the comfort; the positioning of the stereo loudspeakers is good and the sound is satisfactory overall. The on-board computer, for all its general uselessness, is at least not overloaded with buttons. Moreover there is one thing which other firms should copy from BMW, and that is the automatic adjustment of the outside mirror on the passenger's side, so as to sight the kerb and/or wall and/or pole against which one is parking. Small things, but too convenient for so-called competitors not to provide them.

Then there is the facia, with its clear, precise graphics, already mentioned

EDC (electronic damping control) is available as an option. This permits a wide range of shock-absorber settings from "soft" to "hard", depending on driving conditions. This picture shows the 850i in lowered trim, almost totally free from roll.

above. It is always legible in any case, and even more so if the driver is wise enough to use the rheostat to adjust the illumination to his own taste. The said illumination is red, and this is a jolt to the ignorance of those who do not realise its intrinsic suitability. It is an excellent example of how the German firm still remembers and profits from the research carried out during the last World War for military apparatus. I find this very satisfying, and I believe it is a worthy complement to the cloudless efficiency of the biggest and most important of the modern BMWs.

What can one say at the end of a complete test of the 850i, the biggest and most luxurious coupé ever produced in Munich? There are a lot of considerations I could make, but to sum up I can say that in its new flagship BMW has managed successfully to distill over half a century of progress in a direction which has led to it being one of the favourite marques of motoring enthusiasts; that the usual qualities of the Bavarian cars are here raised to the highest levels, and that certain well-known defects of more economical models have been eliminated in this case by the well-tried system of "money no object", or rather the simple provision of resources, and almost unlimited investment. If one wanted to interpret it as a Teutonic translation of the Ferrari-Lamborghini idiom, the 850i would certainly lack some horsepower, and would definitely benefit from the removal of a few hundred kilos (not to mention the removal of the very boring speed limiter). But this is not its vocation. It aspires to the hunting grounds of the Mercedes-Benz 600 SEC, and its additional sportiness leads it to invade, with overweening efficiency, the territory of the super 2+2 coupés for rich, cultured gentlemen, such as the Jaguar XJ-S or the Aston Martin Virage. And it indisputably beats them, and furthermore has less problems connected to reliability, and a competitive price, because its great qualities shine out from amidst an equilibrium of well-balanced shapes and substance which has always been one of BMW's strong points. To sum up, the Bavarians have scored a bull's-eye: and another chapter is opening in the battle with the arch-adversary from Untertürkheim. Awaiting the new 7-Series saloon ...

Considering the category of high displacement sports cars to which it belongs, the 850i has good fuel economy figures, with average consumption (90/120/town cycle) of 13 litre per 100 km.

The BMW 850i is available in the following colors.

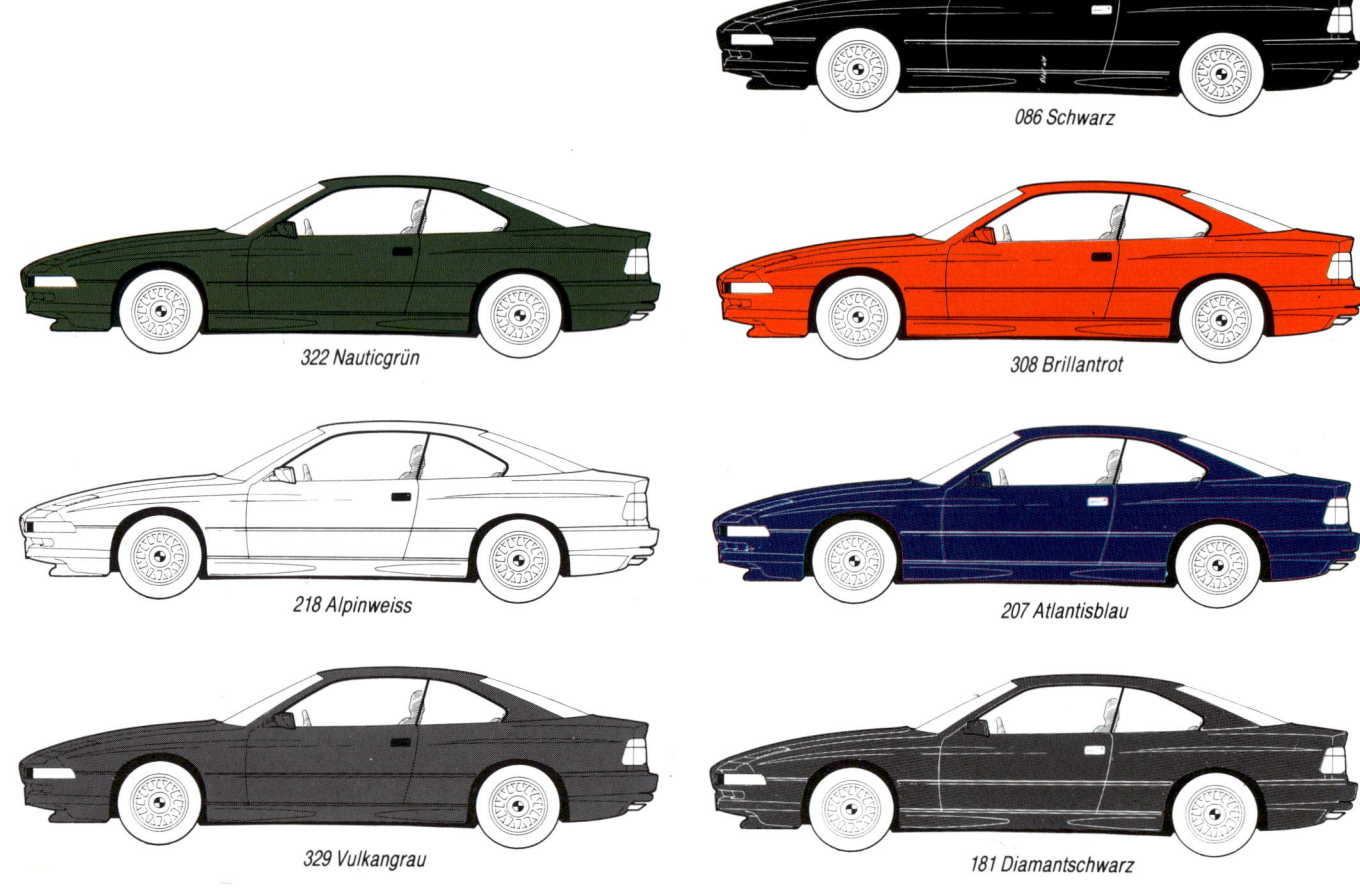

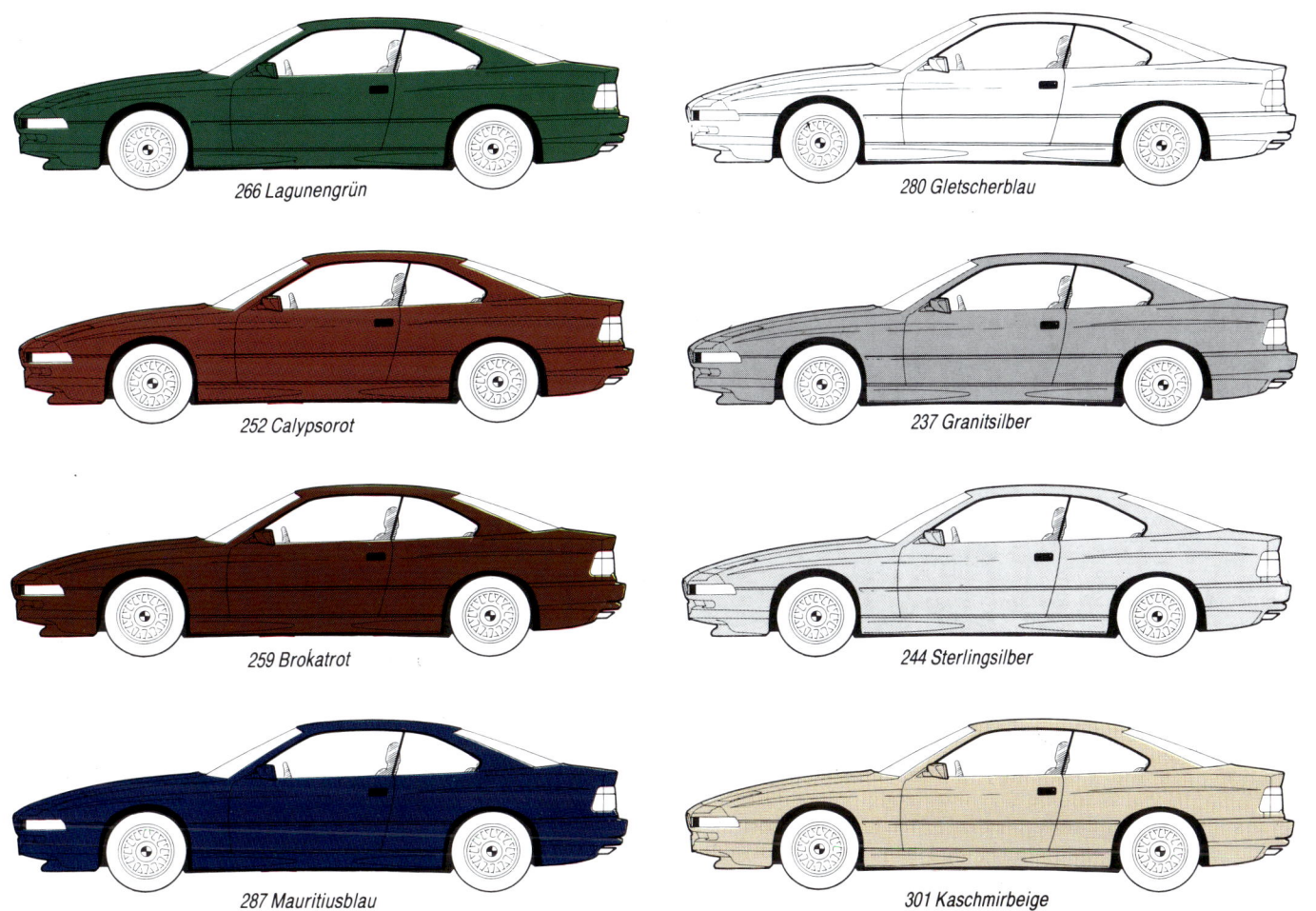

*Automobilia wishes to thank BMW Italia
for their valuable contribution.*